DATE DUE

JAN 2 9 1997			
MAR 0 3 1997	MAR 1 0 2007		
OCT 0 6 1997			
OCT 3 1 1997			
FEB 1 9 1998			
FEB 2 7 1999			
MAR 0 8 2001			
OCT 2 9 2003			
FEB 2 1 2007			

A Tribute to
THE YOUNG AT HEART

JOHN STEPTOE

By Julie Berg

Published by Abdo & Daughters, 4940 Viking Drive, Suite 622, Edina, Minnesota 55435.

Library bound edition distributed by Rockbottom Books, Pentagon Tower, P.O. Box 36036, Minneapolis, Minnesota 55435.

Printed in the United States.

Cover Photo credit: Bettmann Photo
Interior Photo credits Schomberg Center for Research in Black
Culture, Photographs and Prints Division

Edited by Rosemary Wallner

Library of Congress Cataloging-in-Publication Data

Berg, Julie.
    John Steptoe / Julie Berg.
        p.   cm. -- (A Tribute to the Young at Heart)
    ISBN 1-56239-359-6 -- ISBN 1-56239-370-7 (pbk.)
    1. Steptoe, John, 1950-1989 --Juvenile literature.
    2. Authors, American--20th century--biography--Juvenile
    literature. 3. Illustrators--United States--Biography--Juvenile
    literature. 4. Afro-Americans in literature--Juvenile literature.
    [1. Steptoe, John, 1950-1989. 2. Authors, American.
    3. Illustrators. 4. Afro-American--biography.] I. Title.
    II. Series.
    PS3569.T38694Z56   1994
    813' .54--dc20   94-3391
                                         CIP
                                         AC

TABLE OF CONTENTS

A Writer for All Ages and Races

When you look at John Steptoe's books, you know he never forgot what it was like to be a child. His drawings of children's facial expressions and simple stories capture childhood elements without being sentimental.

What makes his books unique are the dialogues aimed at black children. Steptoe was one of the first children's authors to write and illustrate books about and for black children. And he often included positive messages to them. He let them

John Steptoe, artist.

know that their lives were important, that they mattered, and that they could and should follow their dreams.

But even though many of Steptoe's books are about being a black person, they are based on all kinds of family themes to which everyone can relate. This made his books appealing not only to children of all races, but to their parents as well.

Different than the Rest

John Lewis Steptoe was born in Brooklyn, New York, on September 14, 1950. His father, John Oliver, was a trackman for the city transit authority. His mother, Elesteen Steptoe, stayed home and took care of John.

When he was growing up, Steptoe felt he was different than the other children he knew. He did not like to play basketball or baseball. Instead, he liked to draw and paint. He sat in his bedroom for hours and watched how the light made different patterns and shapes on his bedroom wallpaper. His mother noticed his interest in art. She made sure he always had plenty of drawing supplies.

The Young Artist

In 1964 Steptoe enrolled in Manhattan's Art and Design High School. Then he dropped out three months before graduation in 1967. "Art and design was strictly commercial," he said. "It wasn't my thing. I was getting sick on the train fighting all those people when it wasn't that important for me to get where I was going."

John Steptoe as a young artist.

Steptoe found his way to Camden, New Jersey, where he stayed for a few months. Then he moved back to New York where he divided his time between living in Manhattan and Brooklyn. During that time, he explored New York and developed a knowledge of the streets.

Steptoe decided to focus his energies on the one thing he enjoyed most: painting. Seventeen-year-old Steptoe was disciplined for his age. He developed a routine for each painting. First, he covered the canvas with the color burnt umber. "It was like turning off the light and seeing nothing," he said. "Then I started painting in the light."

Self-Discovery

As a young artist, Steptoe was concerned with his ancestral origins. He did not consider himself a typical artist.

"I have been taught Western ideas of what a painter is, what painting is, and that stifles me because I am not a Western man," he once said. "I have never felt I was a citizen of the U.S.A. This country does not speak to me. To be a black man in this society means finding out who I am. So I have got to stay on my own, get out from under induced values and discover who I am at the base. One thing I know: at the base there is blackness. A white man and I can sit together and talk and communicate, but we are different. He is my fellow man, but not my brother. Not many white people can accept that."

Steptoe did not consider himself a typical artist.

Stevie

In addition to drawing, Steptoe liked to read. But he couldn't find many books about black children. So in 1969 he published his first book, *Stevie*. His seven-year-old brother, Charles, was the model for the story's main character.

Stevie is the story of a little boy who comes to stay with Robert and his mother while his own mother goes to work. At first, Robert is resentful that he has to play with and take care of little Stevie. But when Stevie moves away, Robert realizes how much he enjoyed his company.

"The story, the language is not directed at white children," Steptoe explained. "I wanted it to be something black children could read without translating the language, something real which would relate to what a black child would know."

The publication of *Stevie* brought instant recognition to Steptoe. It earned him a gold medal from the Society of Illustrators. The book was chosen a Notable Book by the American Library Association. It appeared on a number of lists of the best books of the year, including *School Library Journal* and *Publishers Weekly*.

The book was even reviewed favorably in *The New York Times*, the most respected book review newspaper in the country. The reviewer, Barbara Novak, said that *Stevie* was "one of the first books set in the ghetto, using black characters, black dialogue and a presumably black life-situation, it certainly stems from black culture. But the simple story the author tells, and . . .illustrates, is of a common experience of young rivalry. Though the author writes and points out of his own blackness, he pushes black identity beyond the 'black is beautiful' stage into a common identity.

Which is as it should be. In fact, one might recommend this book for white children."

Steptoe's career had been launched. And his goal of writing an important story for black children had been realized. The value of the book was obvious. It assured that ghetto children were important enough to be featured in a book.

"I've always considered myself to be primarily a painter," Steptoe revealed. *"Stevie* was my first literary adventure. One of my incentives for getting into writing children's books was the great and disastrous need for books that black children could honestly relate to. I ignorantly created precedents by writing such a book. I was amazed to find out that no one had successfully written a book in the dialogue which black children speak."

What was important was not so much how Steptoe became successful (referring to his background), but the fact that he did do it. He proved that unique books like his could be created and that there was an audience of children who were very much a part of society but who were neglected as far as literature written for and about them.

"It's much more than filling a vacuum," he added. "Black children, all children need good books. Good books are more than a luxury; they are a necessary part of a child's development and it's all of our jobs to see that we all get them."

More Books

Within the next two years (1970 to 1971), Steptoe wrote and illustrated *Uptown* and *Train Ride*, which made *Horn Book* magazine's 1972 Fanfare list. *Train Ride* was among the *New York Time's* outstanding books of 1971. Both books featured black inner-city street talk.

Birthday followed in 1972. It was included in the 1971 to 1972 Children's Book Show mounted by the American Institute of Graphic Arts. That group selected the book as one of twenty American entries to the Biennale of Illustrations.

During that time, Steptoe's daughter, Bweela, and son, Javaka, were born. Because Steptoe was a single father, he had to work on his art at night.

John Steptoe and his son, Javaka.

During the day, he cared for his son and daughter. The studio space where he worked was tidy. But the rest of his apartment was stuffed with photographs he used to help him draw. In 1974 he wrote and illustrated his book *My Special Best Words*, which was a story about his home life.

In 1975, Steptoe shared the Irma Simonton Black Award with author Eloise Greenfield for *She Come Bringing Me That Little Baby Girl*. The award was given by the Bank Street College of Education for an outstanding book for young children combining excellence of text and graphics. The same book was an Honor Book in the competition for the 1975 *Boston Globe Horn Book* Award for Illustration.

Critics praised Steptoe as an innovative author whose works successfully combined positive messages and frankness with a variety of artistic styles. They were especially appreciative of his strong and original characterizations, accurate use of black English, and understanding of children and the way they viewed life.

Reviewers also commented favorably on each stage of Steptoe's development as an artist. Although his stories were sometimes criticized for being weakly constructed and including his personal philosophies, Steptoe was usually praised for the positive messages as well as for the quality of his illustrations.

The Story of the Jumping Mouse

Another well-known book, *The Story of the Jumping Mouse*, was published in 1984. It was a traditional Native American tale retold by Steptoe in lyrical prose and detailed black-and-white drawings. In the story, a mouse journeys to the far-off land he has heard about in legends. In 1985 it was selected as a Caldecott Honor Book.

Mufaro's Beautiful Daughters

Steptoe sometimes used family members as models for the illustrations in his books. In *Mufaro's Beautiful Daughters* (1987), Steptoe's mother was the model for the queen mother.

His nephew, Antoine, was the model for the little boy in the forest, and his daughter, Bweela, was the model for both sisters.

Mufaro's Beautiful Daughters became Steptoe's most well-known book. It won the *Boston Globe Horn Book* Award for Illustration. It also won the Coretta Scott King Award, and the Caldecott Honor medal, the highest award for a children's book.

"The *Boston Globe Horn Book* Award is validation for work that has been ongoing now for almost twenty years," Steptoe said. "During those years, I have learned pride and reasons to be proud. I have also learned that I am able to infuse my work with a loving sense of pride and pass it on to my children and to my readers."

It took Steptoe two-and-a-half years to complete the book. During that time, Steptoe felt he was doing something different than anything else he had created. His abilities as an artist were growing. He began to realize he was capable of creating images that he had wanted to see all his life.

The book's story is based on an ancient African tale of two daughters—Manyara, who is spoiled and unkind, and Nyasha, who is loving and unselfish. In the end, Nyasha's thoughtfulness wins over Manyara's greed. The character's names were taken from an African language called Shona. *Mufaro* means "happy man". *Nyasha* means "mercy". Manyara means ashamed.

Steptoe found the inspiration for his drawings while looking at the ruins of an ancient city in Zimbabwe. He dedicated the book to South African children.

"I wanted to create a book that included some of the things that were left out of my own education about the people who were my ancestors," he said. "I began with the idea of doing a Cinderella story. As I read about the story, what I suspected was confirmed: Cinderella is not just a European story. The Cinderella theme is ancient, and almost every culture has its own unique version of the tale in its storytelling tradition."

His search for information for his book put him in contact with people who became excited about what he wanted to write about. He had never been to southeast Africa. But he was able to find and talk with people there who were willing to share their personal experiences.

"The more I spoke with such people and the more I read, the more reasons I found to be proud of my African ancestors," he said. "I knew in my heart that the history of my race had to be a great history.

But it wasn't easy to defend this belief against the [stories] in history books that the Africans of two or three hundred years ago were not as highly evolved as the Europeans who came to enslave and, later, to colonize them."

Steptoe's friend, Naimani Mutima at the African American Institute, was a great source of information. He gave Steptoe important insights into the role that early historians played in developing false stories that many people still hold about black people.

"When colonialism was at its height," Steptoe said, "certain countries [appointed] scientists to make discoveries that were meant to enhance the reputations of the countries that hired them. In the nineteenth and early twentieth centuries, many countries justified colonialism by claiming they were doing the world a service by helping non-

Europeans fit into the European plan. Needless to say, the [scientist] who discovered that civilization existed in Africa before it was occupied by Europeans would not have been popular with his employers. Also, scientists who made unpopular discoveries were not likely to be paid.

"This is why, when the ruins in Zimbabwe were first discovered, they were declared to be of European origin," he added. "It was impossible for Europeans to think that an African people could have been as clever, skilled, and industrious as the builders of this ancient city must have been. It is now known that the city is of African origin."

The evidence of past glory in the Zimbabwe ruins made Steptoe think hard. A people who got together to build a city that lasted for hundreds of years must have been organized. Also, people don't build a city just to look at it. So, they must have been doing something that motivated them.

Artifacts found at the ruins suggested the inhabitants were involved in trade with the Orient as well as among themselves. All this suggested a society working together for a common end.

"Like any society," Steptoe said, "they must have had rules to govern themselves. They must have had families. And those families raised children to follow the rules that made their way of life possible. The story in Africa told me that my ancestors were probably very much like my own family. Once I made that connection, I knew who my characters were and that they had dignity and grace. I also knew they cared for one another as a family, for better or worse."

Though *Mufaro's Beautiful Daughters* was said to be based on an African tale, Steptoe likes to think that he modeled the story on a world ancestral tale. "Even though I fully understand

and support the reason for making this distinction," he said, "I'd like it to be known that I did not write and illustrate a special-interest book. I hope I have made a statement that is even greater than my discovery of reasons to be proud of African ancestors. I hope the book is also a statement of brotherhood in the wide world into which I was born."

Steptoe working in his studio.

Proud of His Heritage

Steptoe was proud of his black heritage, and of his publishing success. He often encouraged others of his race to reach for their dreams.

"There is something I want to be said about me," he once stated. "I am not an exception to the rule among my race of people. I am the rule. By that I mean there are a great many others like me where I come from. There are hundreds of thousands of young people who want to accomplish something important with their lives and who need understanding and encouragement to seek the opportunities open to them. That [the readers] have understood and appreciated what I have put into *Mufaro's Beautiful Daughters* gives me hope that children who are still caught in the frustration of being black and poor in America will be encouraged to love themselves enough to accomplish the dreams I know are in their hearts."

Though he was successful, people often asked Steptoe when he would "grow up" and write an adult book. But Steptoe always thought that his writing had value for everyone, not just children.

"If you said there was a particular kind of person, on a particular sort of a level, who has to write for children, as opposed to a kind of person who has to write for adults, would you say the same thing about a surgeon who's going to operate on a child?" he stated. "It has to be a surgeon. It has to be a full-blown person who knows what it is he's doing and who knows how to do it. That is what I feel I've been doing for the last twenty years of my career."

When he wasn't working, Steptoe enjoyed going to museums and theaters and listening to music. He also enjoyed watching "Star Trek" on TV. Steptoe had his own style of dress and even designed and sewed his own clothes. He died on August 28, 1989, at the age of 38 of complications from AIDS.

Follow Your Heart

John Steptoe believed that everyone should follow his or her own heart. He encouraged children to work hard at whatever was important to them and not to allow anyone to keep them from their dreams. And he encouraged black children everywhere to be proud of their heritage.

Dorothy Briley, his editor of seventeen years, put it best when she said: "Like the character in *Jumping Mouse*, John wished to reach beyond his circumstances and share with children his vision of a better world. Through his books he wanted to share his conviction that African-Americans have reason to be proud. All of his books are about family and the struggle to maintain dignity in a world that he many times perceived as being hostile."

Books by John Steptoe

Stevie (1969)

Uptown (1970)

Train Ride (1971)

Birthday (1972)

My Special Best Words (1974)

Marcia (1976)

Daddy Is a Monster. . .Sometimes (1980)

Jeffrey Bear Cleans Up His Act (1983)

The Story of Jumping Mouse: A Native
   American Legend (1984)

Mufaro's Beautiful Daughters: An African Tale (1987)

Baby Says (1988)